POETRY NOW

THE POETRY WORKOUT

Edited by Kerrie Pateman

First published in Great Britain in 1995 by
POETRY NOW
1-2 Wainman Road, Woodston,
Peterborough, PE2 7BU

HB ISBN 1 85731 447 6
SB ISBN 1 85731 452 2

FOREWORD

Although we are a nation of poetry writers we are accused of not reading poetry and not buying poetry books: after many years of listening to the incessant gripes of poetry publishers, I can only assume that the books they publish, in general, are books that most people do not want to read.

Poetry should not be obscure, introverted, and as cryptic as a crossword puzzle: it is the poet's duty to reach out and embrace the world.

The world owes the poet nothing and we should not be expected to dig and delve into a rambling discourse searching for some inner meaning.

The reason we write poetry (and almost all of us do) is because we want to communicate: an ideal; an idea; or a specific feeling. Poetry is as essential in communication, as a letter; a radio; a telephone, and the main criteria for selecting the poems in this anthology is very simple: they communicate.

Faced with hundreds of poems and a limited amount of space, the task of choosing the final poems was difficult and as editor one tries to be as detached as possible (quite often editors can become a barrier in the writer-reader exchange) acting as go between, making the connection, not censoring because of personal taste.

In this anthology over one hundred and thirty poems are presented to the reader for their enjoyment.

The poetry is written on all levels; the simple and the complex both having their own appeal.

The success of this collection, and all previous *Poetry Now* anthologies, relies on the fact that there are as many individual readers as there are writers, and in the diversity of styles and forms there really is something to please, excite, and hopefully, inspire everyone who reads the book.

CONTENTS

RUNNER

Mind over Matter if that is the case -
Watch what you're doing and stay in the race . . .
Runners in front - Runners behind,
Keep up a steady pace and you will
Reach the Finish Line.
Up over Hill - and down over Dale,
Retaining your strength against the uncoming gale.
The Runners in front seem to be going in haste . . .
'But don't you worry they might lose their pace!'
Finish Line seems so far away,
'But you will keep going strong all the way . . .'
Feet are getting sore now with having run so far -
'But whatever you do - don't stop for a Jar.'
The end is in sight - not far to go now,
Just a few hundred yards and you're home -
Safe and dry . . . !

Jerry Moore

TRANSACTIONAL ANALYSIS

Lie on my couch.
Reveal to me
Your deepest thoughts,
Your history.
Find the reasons for your insanity.

Transactional analysis
Strips your soul bare,
Finds the child
Still inside your mind.

Transactional analysis
Drives you crazy,
Splits open those sores
Like the cool, quick slice
Of a surgeon's knife.

Transactional analysis
Leaves you reeling,
Raw and bleeding.
A private crucifixion.
Life blood flowing
From your veins.

Lie on my couch.
Reveal to me
Your deepest thoughts,
Your history.
Find the reasons for your insanity.

Transactional analysis
Resurrects your pain,
Turns you upside-down and back again
To the harsh bright light of day.
A world without reason,
A cacophony of pain.
Transactional analysis will drive you insane.

Irene Hrynkow

DAMN DIETS

Dieting's a modern fad, it takes the land by storm,
It keeps you fit and healthy, so the magazines inform.

There's a diet for every age-group, for every shape and size.
The common aim, a trimmer frame, is every dieter's prize.
I've tried grapefruit, no fat, steak and eggs, the Cambridge, F-Plan too,
Seven-day wonder diets, and beastly bars you chew.

I bought a leotard, tracksuit, tights, legwarmers and all,
With all this keep-fit gear to hand, I'm really on the ball.
I've bounced upon a trampoline, done aerobics on the floor.
An hour's daily exercise - I haven't time for more.
I've been jogging every morning, done press-ups every night:
The kids think it's hysterical, they say it's quite a sight.
Entertainment value, is it? Call it healthy? At a pinch.
Despite relentless exercise, I've scarcely lost an inch.

Now, the tracksuit's great for lounging, the leotard's done its stuff,
Go hang the health obsession, I feel I've had enough.
What use for cast-off legwarmers? Just push a French loaf through,
Put them by the front door, and they'll stop a draught or two.

Damn diets - let others try them, my health-craze days are done.
I'll opt for fat and forty, still the children's tubby mum.

Elspeth Wallington

THE FITNESS THINKER

Today in the mirror I found,
That my middle is too big around.
My skin is too taught,
And my breath all too short, -
And my energy does not abound!

Now I suppose I feel somewhat ashamed,
I've decided tis time that I changed.
I must lose all this weight,
Yes that would be great,
To get fit is what must be arranged!

So where should I make this new start,
I suppose it should be with my heart.
I'll go down to the gym,
And sweat till I'm thin,
But then, I'd probably just fall apart!

I know, I'll go for a run,
Now that sounds like it could be fun.
But then, I'm too overweight for that type of gait,
So I'll just think, while I sit in the sun!

I suppose I could take up Tai Chi,
Now that sounds about right for me,
It's graceful and slow, but then again, no,
I think I'll just sit here and see!

Perhaps I should go on a diet,
Now that really would be quite a riot,
What me, cut down on my food,
No I'm far too shrewd,
I'll just think in the peace and the quiet!

Now the answer to all this it seems,
Lies not in these wild wreckless dreams,
I'll just go for a walk,
With my wife and just talk,
And then maybe we'll buy some ice creams!

R E Pearshouse

YOGA

I fancied taking exercise
but thought it much too hard.
To do aerobics or to jog,
to get rid of my lard.
Then I saw a notice
saying yoga classes here,
It looked so slow and gentle
I signed up without fear.

We started off with breathing,
how to do it right.
Then to stretch our muscles,
to loosen all that's tight.
We bent and stretched
this way and that,
stood up, sat down
lay on the mat.
Twisted round and back again,
how my idle muscles ached.
As I lay shattered on the ground,
I thought *I've made a big mistake*.

But then she said now just relax,
and let your breath out with a hiss.
Let my voice wash over you.
Calming music, utter bliss.

Sylvia Dodds

COMPETITION

Red, green, blue, yellow,
- tingling, churning colours of vests and shorts
of one hundred boys about to race:
Two sons tense and poised,
My adrenalin pumping both for them and
for past glories chased,
- now just memories, dressed in cobwebs of time.

I always considered competition healthy,
- Perhaps an integral ingredient of survival.
After all, even communists compete.
Whether it is necessary is I suppose
a question of degree.

But, as to being *best*;
How many winners are indeed best?
And, how many losers fall short?
How important was the competition,
And what purpose did it serve?
After the sweat and tears
Did a smile return?

Ivan Sanders

1-3

You packed your kit in bag (and hope)
and, driving there, rehearsed the strokes.
You dressed for play and swung your hips,
mentally scrolling vital tips:
hit a full length, impose your will,
control the tee, don't rush to kill.

In the strained warm-up you rightly
sought mobility, and certain touch.

The match under way, you did the lot -
drove, volleyed, lobbed, boasted and dropped,
rallied, attacked, retrieved the ball -
nothing was left to chance at all.

He won two games, you the third;
he led in the fourth - you battled hard.

But, though you ran and ran and ran,
this squash match, pal, went down the pan.

Wes Ashwell

IT MAKES SENSE

It pays to look after your body,
It works, whether you like it or not.
Don't feed it all sorts of rubbish,
And keep off the cigarettes and pot.
Exercise, no doubt, is good for it,
But don't overdo it, take care!
Like everything else, moderation!
Or you'll finish up in a wheelchair.
When you're young you relish the challenge,
To push it, as far as you can.
That's all very well, when you're twenty,
When you feel like a superman.
When you get old, you'll certainly realise,
There's a limit to what you can do.
Make hay while the sun is still shining,
Don't regret if you can't see it through.
Don't forget, nothing gained, if not ventured.
Now the rest of it's all up to *you.*

Selwyn L Thomas

THE PEACOCK

I used to be fit
all muscles and brawn
Out for a jog
A lap of the park
Squatting and thrusting
Till the sweat came pouring
Down at the gym
Lifting the weights
Pulling twenty a time
Just pumping iron
Then around the pool
My pectorals flexing
Or swimming about
My biceps bulging
Strutting about
A lady's warning
God how boring!

Simon Dent

IN APPRECIATION OF COMMON SENSE

The eating of butter makes you fat,
but the lack of it will make you sad.
And too much milk - the calcium sack,
will only make your ulcers bad.
And these slimline beauties in the daily rags,
who pass for normal make me mad!

Krystyna Lejk

WATERSHED

When I was nine and seventy
Not many months agone
My energy was boundless
And at heavy work I shone.

There were times I found it tiring
And had to pause and rest
But I stubbornly refused all help
And kept on, with the best.

But now I'm into eighty
I look at jobs and say
'I don't think I could manage that'
And slowly creep away.

So why this change at eighty?
It's a funny age, I'm told.
My physique's as good as ever.
It's my mind that's growing old.

Bill Johnson

WALKING, JUST WALKING

Walking, just walking
Talking, sitting, admiring,
Taking photographs and taking time
We have all day and one road
Who could ask for anything more.

Company, laughter and walking shoes
And a lighthouse on the horizon
Out of reach yet a good view awaits,
On the mountain around the corner
There is perfection in the camera lens.

Superlatives fall like gentle rain
As the beer my thirst demands
Refreshes and relaxes like the touch
Of your arms around my shoulders,
But now the darkness steals the page
And of further exercise I dare not tell.

Ian Ambrose

FIT ME?

I'm hardly what you call fit,
But I'm not unhealthy either.
Slimfast? I won't touch a bit.
Fat or thin? I'm neither.

I've strength in every limb,
In my body there's adequate power,
But I've never worked out in the gym,
Not even for half an hour!

I don't swim, but I ride
And I walk round the house everyday.
Strong men? I hide!
Gladiators? No Way!

OK so sport's not for me,
But healthy eating's more my game.
Oh Gosh! It's time for tea;
Burgers and chips again!

Hannah Marder (11)

FIT FOR NOTHING

I used to play tennis, badminton, squash
Thinking that jogging was a load of old tosh
But now that I'm older and losing my puff
A walk with the dog is more than enough
I even tried yoga to clear my head
'Think beautiful thoughts' the tutor said
But try as I may I had no success
Just kept right on thinking of problems instead

As old age creeps on and my bones start to creak
The thought of exercise makes my legs feel all weak
My waistline has thickened, my thighs look like logs
To be truthful my figure has gone to the dogs
But every morning come rain, sleet or snow
Round the park with my collie I go

My diet is varied with plenty of fibre
And I only smoke twenty a day
Each evening I partake of the whisky or wine
As in front of the TV I stay
But my job keeps me active, my dog keeps me fit
And I rarely take time off from work

So all fitness fanatics wherever you are
Enjoying aerobics or a jog in the dark
Think of me relaxing with a whisky and fags
Or taking a leisurely stroll round the park
For all's said and done, life is far too brief
To stretch your limbs to the limit and give your muscles such grief
So give your body a rest and let your mind run free
And you'll feel so much better, just wait and see.

Angela Edwards

SPIRITUAL EXERCISES

Joggers for Jesus
Pounding the pavement
(A born again jogger
Is a terrible sight)

Joggers for Jesus
Trot past the temple
Chant as you pant
Gouranga be happy
Callisthenics for Krishna

Joggers for Jesus
Sweep by the synagogue
The rabbi is leading
Yoga for Yahweh

Joggers for Jesus
Pass the pagoda
A gong is sounding
Bobsleighs for Buddha

Joggers for Jesus
Close their eyes
As the Natural Joggers
Proudly go by
(A born again
Naturist
Jogger
Is a terrible sight).

Alex Kashko

PERSEVERANCE

Been on all sorts of diets
Low fat food *I've tried it*,
But it didn't really work
As hunger pangs still lurked
So I decided to get tough with myself
Instead of having fat that looked more like a shelf
I would exercise daily for an hour or so
Pretending the fat is my foe
Up, down and twist around
Touch my toes, reaching for the ground
On the spot running is quite hard
It would be easier to do it around the backyard
But still I persevere
Shedding sweat and occasional tear
But I think it might be worth it in the end
Getting rid of my load and not having to pretend
No more baggy jumpers to wear
Just clothes that flatter and show flair
Head held up high as I walk down the street
Knowing I can have the occasional treat. Yippee!

J A Burkill

DREAM FITNESS

I really am a keen fitness fanatic -
About other people's health and trim I mean,
I like to see them swim and jogging along
I do that too - but only when I dream.

I see myself exercise and joining in a run
And my pudding shape trimming down to lean,
But I get another inspiration to jot down
And once again am lost in worlds of dream.

One day I will join the joggers - when not
Composing odes and writing stories clean,
My hands and brain are supple and so fit
One day the rest will match - till then I dream.

Gwen Mason

UNTITLED

They say I'll feel good but all I feel is sweat,
My penance for all the food that I ate,
I'm panting and groaning and down on my knees,
To banish away those damn calories,
My legs are wrapped up in amazing contortions,
To make up for last nights amazing big portions,
Jazzercise, boxercise, cardiofunk,
Toffee fudge ice-cream with thick chocolate chunk,
I'll step up and down to the beat of some song,
Convincing myself I look good in my thong,
I'm squeezing away at my *buns* till I scream,
The only buns I want are covered in cream,
Every American superstar under the sun,
Is here to show me how it's done;
So maybe I'll save myself all of the trouble,
And invest in a bloody body double.

Nancy Ivison

POEM TO SLIM

If I eat fit and keep fit
Never a skirt seam will I split
I'll think when I bite
Of things I would like
To wear but won't fit in
Due to food that I pile in
I'll drink lots of water
Eat veg that I ought to
Exercise daily
And soon then well maybe
I'll feel good and I'll look good
When my clothes fit, as they should
My bum will be smaller
My confidence taller
So this is my aim
To lose weight, not to gain
To tone and to slim
Against flab I shall win!

Jenny Ness

BODY IN MOTION

Keeping fit is a real big issue these days
Of that there is no doubt
The younger ones are more fitness minded
The old don't know what it's all about

You don't have to go to classes
Or get an exercise bike
You can do a few minutes at home every day
If that is what you would like

But none at all is not very good for you
So get up and have a go
If not when you're old, your joints will seize up
And your movements will get really slow

But if you're on diet as most are these days
Exercise is a must
To tone up those flabby muscles
Whilst eating just a crust

You can exercise while doing your veg
Or washing at the sink
A little a day, keeps the Doctor away
And that's a good thing, don't you think?

Eva Agnes Emma Stanley

A FORM OF TORTURE

I'm a masochist who toes the line
A modern woman in a modern time
I don't use whips, a rope or chain
I'm into a different kind of pain.

Hundreds of people giving it a try
For reasons that we know why
The media shout out its name
To everyone sane or insane.

Twice a week I sweat and toil
Trying to be loyal
With others who follow suit
Hoping it will bear fruit.

Tee-shirts, leggings, leotards and trainers
Wearing clothes that don't restrain us
Music playing all around
Bodies moving to the sound.

Our teacher asks us how we feel
It's hard to talk when the pain's so real
So all we do is grit our teeth
And pray for the final release.

I hope you've guessed what I do
And everything that I go through
You'll recognise this poem's not a farce
When you learn it's about my exercise class.

To all the ones like me
Who are striving to get healthy
Just remember the golden rule
An unhealthy person is a fool.

Doreen Wallace

WEIGHTY PROBLEM

It seems like only yesterday,
I was so slim, I'd blow away.
But now you should see, what I weigh,
I truly don't know what to say.

All my bumps and ridges show,
I've tried every diet, that I know.
After that it's still a blow,
For all I do is further grow.

I eat salads, by the score,
Do my exercises on the floor.
Sometimes I feel so very sore,
Feel I just can't do any more.

I'm as elegant as a stampeding moose,
Waddling along, like a Christmas goose.
My clothes are either tight or loose,
Think that I am, of not much use.

You're cuddly! people say to me,
(I'll hit the next one! Wait and see).
Slim is everything I want to be,
Just like a model, out of page three.

Denise Sanders

NO PAIN, NO GAIN

Pumping, iron, for fun and pleasure,
Sit on a beach, to pose at leisure.
Watch all the glances, you will share.
Flex your muscles, without a care
A Poser's paradise, you will see.
A body beautiful, you will be.
Tanned and bronzed, like the great Adonis
Don't look now, the spotlight's on us.
Back at the gym, you'll feel the strain
The sun tan's gone, it's time to train.
Because as the saying goes, no pain, no gain.

Mark Lambourne

WORKOUT AM EARLY

Listen very carefully from the changing room
And you can tell it's a serious business.
Piston limbs work along water; progress
Echoes like paddle-wheels, up to
A swirling surge of turns.

Look, as you try to slide yourself in
And keep clear water behind you.
Utilitarian costumes cling to toning muscle;
Circulations visibly improve
Under an envy of varying tans.

Hearts and lungs increase capacity
With prescribed breaths taken efficiently,
Checking slyly sideways what lengths
We go to, all of us swimming
Against the tide.

David Goodall

SING A SONG OF FITNESS

Sing a song of fitness,
The sight will make you cry,
If you want to weight less,
Look pleasing to the eye,
Give up the salt and sugar,
And your greasy fry,
And eat your veg and salad,
You will see the reason why.

You will live much longer,
Your far too young to die,
You will look so sexy,
Catch all the young men's eye,
You will look alluring in everything you wear,
You will be so stunning, everyone will stare.

You will look sleek and slim dear,
Not like a pink blancmange,
There's no need to shed a tear, dear,
The podge will soon be gone,
You will feel much fitter,
In everything you do,
You'll also run much quicker
And look good in something new.

You can start Aerobics, run a marathon or two,
Give up all your smoking,
Your lungs will see you through,
You can paint your nails red,
And your lips the selfsame hue,
Life will be much better,
And love will be more true.

Linda Skrzypczak

HAPPY-HEALTHY LIFE

Bed before midnight,
Wake at six,
Meditation - exercise,
Fresh juice squeeze.
No tensions - no worry,
It's not the world's end,
You do your job the best you can.

No hurry - no rush,
Meditate - relax,
Nothing you have to do,
A must is only death.
Plenty fruit and vegas,
Some milk, not too much cheese,
Animals are friends so -
No meat.

Happy life is there,
The simplest is the best,
Exercise your body
Then have some rest.
Dealing with the people
No need to be mad,
No need to be sad,
No problem exist -
All is in your head.

Marina Montina

CALORIES

For my tea tonight
I shall have a baked potato
Topped with grated reduced fat cheese
Together with a fresh green salad
All washed down by a sugar free orange drink
(Only four cals per 100mls)
Then I'll have plenty of room for a big helping
Of treacle pudding and custard.

Brian Eatherton

FIT FOR NOTHING

There was a young woman called Lynn
Who felt the urge to be thin
Though her leotard was tight
She decided she might
Give *Work Out To Music* a spin

To the Leisure Centre she trotted
And with Tuesday nights got quite besotted
So hooked on the craze
She went all the days
Now she's an *aeroboholic*.

Joanne Davies

HEALTHY LIVING

I was fairly energetic, but I didn't run or jog
I took my daily exercise going walkies with my dog.
When on our country rambles, I thought of modern farming ways
Of how they treated vegetables with pesticides and sprays.

So I got me an allotment to grow my peas and beans
I added carrots, parsnips, beet, and lots of healthy greens.
I've got strawberries, raspberries, logans. I even have a vine
A friend came to pick the grapes to make organic wine.
There are gooseberries, currants black and red, onions and shallots,
I've planted thyme and rosemary and other herbs in pots.

The compost heap is there as well. There isn't any waste.
Expensive veggies bought in shops just don't compare in taste.
With taties, radish, lettuce, sweetcorn and celery
I think I've found the answer to living healthily.
I have to get up early to water and to hoe
But it's worth the extra effort for the lovely things I grow.

Joan Ierston

TAKE HEED THEN

'Early to bed and early to rise'
Are words simple and wise
And moderate eating and drinking
          Keep you well
          As you've heard tell.
          Take heed then!

'You are old, Father William' the young man said . . .
'And yet you incessantly stand on your head.
Do you think at your age it is right?'
To stand on your head is the yoga view
And certainly this is of great benefit to you.
          Take heed then!

M Wood

WHAT IS HEALTH?

Yoga is my answer,
And a kindly, wise guru
Teaching the need for balance
In all we think and do.

Health, I have discovered
Means becoming *whole* -
A perfect integration
Of body, mind and soul.

Anne Finnis

VEGGIE TWILIGHT

My hair is white now I'm a gran,
My diet full of antioxidants and bran,
Can this be the girl whose diet was horrific?
Whose delight in chips and chocolate was prolific!
Since I grew old and became a veggie,
Meat and junk foods make me edgy.
I feel sixteen and walk for miles.
My life is changed and full of smiles.
It's never too late to change your ways
Eat a healthy diet and lengthen your days.

Gloria McKay

PARTY POETICAL BROADSIDE

As a nation we are worried
'bout good health of economics;
Let's make Docs' Bill *poor relation*,
Lest we dupe acute or chronic
Future, ailing to our hurried
Policies which push fake tonics
Con-by-hack who, potion failing,
Exorcise their fit demonics
(*liquid burn* we runs full-curried!)
H E A R T mnemonic:
Health Ends After Rushing Your Turn
To become deaths' supersonic,
Dead-tape victim, bread 'n' burried
By plagued civiserve *bubonics*
In their rivalry-power dictums
To old gods Brave Electronic
Hospitals' surge turgerries -
Palecoat zombiephobics -
Carers . . . in rebalanced cost
Of a fading, old-tile clinic
Where politicians' rent book tallied -
Blame upon ill-met semantics,
And the shameless, jobless scare-cranks
Bravely waging *Foul!* pedantics . . .
Paying quack-ducks' bill we're bullied,
No more moaning histrionics;
'We in The House . . . arselick to gills!' . . .
While us *mob-wincers*, we're pathetic!

And that was a party poetical broadside
On behalf of the Injured Party.

James Parry

GARDEN OF EDEN

The world is sick and it must die,
So hear the *Armageddon* cry.
We left the Garden, heed the warning,
We, are sick and we, must die.

Pollution, guns and menace reign,
And drugs to heal the hurting brain.
So leave us dead, we didn't care,
To see, to feel, to know, the pain.

But stop! and touch the earth a while,
And share her warmth, her mother-smile,
For as the herb is Everything,
So Words are made, the world to sing.

Virginia

PLANT MEDICINE

What do we know of plant medicine?
Can we eat those lovely Roses?
Follow me and I will take you back to Moses
With few Doctors around the ill in despair
Looked towards medicine indeed
Moses was sad but felt quite glad
To say *Eat you of the coriander seed*
What is this seed and what does it do?
Well we know it helps digestion
Well what of chuppatties and what of tomatoes?
Well we know them as plant medicine
With few doctors in sight - to ease their plight
The Lord worked wonders you see
He was right on hand and with one command
Ordered
Eat you of the coriander seed.
Our system needs acid our system needs balance
Tomatoes helps tummies while chupatties help mummies
Resist the ills of the day
And what of cucumber its colour so green
Surely that is no good at all
While that plays its part taking oxygen to the heart
And you don't have to eat the seeds at all
What then of lettuce such a tasteless wee bite
I was made to eat it while young
Lettuce relaxes the intestine and stops feeling tired
Gives a spring in our step every time
So that being said plan wisely ahead
And you will always feel so young.

Rosaleen O'Brien

THE JOGGER

Setting off - no turning back -
Out along the beaten track
Byways, grassland, country lane
Hopefully no sign of rain,
Filling lungs with clean fresh air
Breezes blowing through the hair

Adrenaline now starts to flow
Encouraging the will to go,
On and on the footsteps pound
Trainers covering the ground
Exercising every part
Muscles, limbs and beating heart

Stress and rigours of the day
Disappear along the way,
Thoughts of work all left behind
Forge ahead with peace of mind
All alone along each mile,
Achievement makes it so worthwhile

Then at last the home retreat
Time to halt those trusting feet
Their task has been a job well done
Accomplishing the scheduled run,
Vibrating ego fit and well,
How far next time? Well, who can tell!

Evelyn Jones

AN ESSAY ON BRAN

(Long) after Alexander Pope

Presume not Mind or Memory to scan:
The proper study of mankind is bran.
As Caesar knew, before he crossed the Tiber;
The man of steel needs more than *moral* fibre!

The hairy Gaul at war will not forgo
His luscious bowl of greasy *escargot,*
He spies those Roman crew-cuts and he quakes -
Undone by early morning Weeta-flakes.

In modern as in ancient times, it holds:
A dietary thought-police enfolds
Our world, our worship, grinning while they'll give
Us longer lives, but little cause to live.

The regimented rule of brankind spreads,
New Spartans shake the brains from sleepy-heads.
They tend their bodies, wasting not a minute;
The earth is theirs and theirs is all that's in it.

Whatever else they live for I can't guess,
Just mindless prolongation here, unless
They hope to breed another race as dull,
Who only breathe to scoff of bran their full.

I'll try and learn (although it be a wrench!)
A lifestyle from these fibrous übermensch.
Dull all my senses, moralise my plate.
And some day trust to bran, and not to Fate.

Conrad Brunström

ODE TO A CHOCOLATE BAR

There you lie, I feel your tempting game,
I should be strong, instead I long to lift you close to me
And smell the warmth, and sweetness of your sensuous shape,
Beneath its gaudy wrapper, that hints of lands from whence
you came.

Your dusky beauty comes in many shapes and guises,
Full of mystery, and sweet surprises,
I know my weakness will result in surplus pounds,
Each creamy mouthful will, turn into mounds of roly-poly fat,
But I am hooked!

Dawn finds me on my regular jog, I puff and blow
Along each street sometimes I even take the dog
To help me boost my flagging feet.
Grated carrot, low fat spread, fish and white meat, not much red.

I've tried so hard to toe the line, but I am weak,
You must be mine.
Perhaps tomorrow I will try,
If *only* I can pass you by!

Jean Stenton

WORKING FOR FUN

Work the weight stacks
Pile them up higher
I'll pass the limit
Body won't tire
Living for the workouts
That's what I do

Pulling my arms right down
Taking all the strain
Lungs are gasping
Throats red raw
But keep on hitting it
Always ready for more

Time for a break now
Wipe my pecs down
Check out the girls
I'm on the prowl
Firing out smiles
Waiting for a sign
That's a classy option
She could be mine

But turn away smoothly
And dig deep again
This is what I was born for
Flexing beyond the pain
Welcome to the Weights Room
This is my only domain.

Richard Page

FOLLOWING THE FITNESS PLAN

Ruled by the tape measure, weighed down by the scales
Diet books and videos boosting their sales
Trying out a new one with all that it entails
When hoping to reduce your span
Just start following the fitness plan

Give up cakes and biscuits, chocolate is out
Fatty treats and full cream you will do without
Calories are counted, resist a binge-ing bout
Concentrate on fibre and bran
Boldly following the fitness plan

First exercise daily with gentle campaigns
Don't begin in a hurry, enthusiasm wanes
But little and often will cure aches and pains
We want every woman and man
Stiffly following the fitness plan

Walk, jog, or take a hike, see the countryside
Step aerobics, swimming, an exercise bike ride
Watch your body taking shape, viewing it with pride
You won't end up an also ran
Gamely following the fitness plan.

Cut back on alcohol, give up the weed
A healthy way of life is all you will need
Make a promise to yourself and you will succeed
Be fit? Live longer? Yes you can
Wisely following the fitness plan.

Margery Peloe

CATCH 22

Half a million lycra clad joggers,
A million elastic band legs,
Half a million jolted backs,
A million pounds to the NHS.

Through need to achieve that ideal physique
Through vanity and to follow the trend.

Half a million fried breakfasts,
A million pounds of excess fat,
Half a million premature deaths,
A million bereaved families.

And the question,
Is it better to die early, yet happy
Or be wheelchair bound and depressed?

Alistaire Storme

I DIET MY WAY!

They think that I'm crazy but why should I care
When I see them in clothes that strain to contain
All the pizzas and pastries and pies.

'You're not eating veggies again!' They will laugh
As they turn up their nose and frown as they drown
In their coffee and cola and cream.

They say that I worry but that is my right
When our foods have been sprayed and pumped up with junk
That's not normal or natural or new.

So I'll let them make fun of me, call me a crank
But I'll stand by my views and smile for a while
Feeling happy and healthy and high.

Susan Kelland

THE KEEP FIT INSTRUCTOR

Get those muscles working, I'll train you into health
I won't charge a penny, you can keep your wealth.
When I'm finally through, you'll be as fit as can be
Then you will be thankful, your trainer was me.

Jog on the spot right now, as fast as you can go,
Get those knees up higher, be sure to point the toe.
Press ups next, then tennis, for an hour or two,
You'll sweat off a stone dear, before I am through with you.

Now do your aerobics, after that the trampoline,
Stop your rotten moaning, I am not being mean.
That's all for today, tomorrow we start once more,
But I shall stay on the couch dear, and let you keep the floor.

Carole Horsman

BAD NIGHT IN HELL

As I was led to the room
The doors opened, the noise hit me
There were groans, grunts
Bodies heaving objects up and down
Agony bestowed on the faces of some
Self induced torture, bulging muscles
Sweating vests and brows
Do I have to do that
I amble tentatively, am I in hell I ask myself
I must be a masochist
Self inflicting my body to the limits
Here goes up, down, up, down
Push, heave, grunt, groan,
Sweat, pant, run, stop, squat, run
Knees up, arms up, running on the spot
Press ups, pull ups
Gasp, pant, wheeze, heart attack
Ringing in my ears ringing, ringing
Thank Christ for that what a nightmare
Time to get up
The ringing of the alarm clock greets me
Seems like music to my ears
Eggs, bacon, fried bread, sausages
And perhaps a mushroom or two
All that exercise has made me quiet hungry.

Ian Buddle

THE FANATIC

I knew that one day it would happen,
And for me it seemed terribly rare,
Losing weight was a farce,
Till I slipped in the dark,
And bounced down each bloody stair.

The doctor suggested I jog twice a week,
I didn't think that wise at all,
He said, 'Don't worry mate,
The flab round your waist
Will act as a cushion if you fall.'

Each footstep resounded like thunder,
And the pavement must have been very frail,
For as my feet hit,
The slabs cracked and they split,
Playing havoc with the damn rictor-scale.

That dieting lark was a bummer,
I was given new *Flab Flop* to drink,
But my weight grew and grew,
This is crap I just knew,
So I brought it all back in the sink.

And now when I see those fanatics,
With track suits and trainers and things,
Carry on and you'll see,
You'll end up just like me,
Playing the harp with a halo and wings!

Stephen Griffiths

MY TROUSERS ARE TOO TIGHT

I'm 31 years old and my trousers are too tight
It seems my waistline has grown overnight
There is a large bulge where my stomach used to be
Is someone playing a joke on me?
You see I look down and I can't see my toes
Every time I look I'm sure this lump grows
It gets in the way when I bend down
When I walk it casts a shadow on the ground
It follows me wherever I go.
I wish I knew what was making it grow
Where it has come from I just can't say
Don't think it was there the other day
It seems to have grown right before my eyes
Or maybe it's due to no exercise!

Steve King

ANOTHER DIET

So
You're on another diet
Yes
I think that I might try it
As you still seem
            to make a meal
                    out of
                            everything.

Andrew Rumsey

A FIT BITCH

'I'm really into fitness now,' she said.
'I'm really into fitness -
It does wonders for my head!'

'I can think so very clearly,
I can do my work so well,
Though I don't mean to sound boastful,
It's improved my sex as well!'

I couldn't really challenge her,
I didn't really know,
But she made me feel so flabby,
And so sexless, and so slow.

I looked straight in her sparkling eye,
Puffed out my sagging chest,
And since she'd made me want to bitch,
I bitched my very best!

'So, you're really into fitness then?' I said.
'You might be into fitness now -
You won't be when you're dead!'

Ruth Fair Stewart

AEROBIC JUNKIES

Warm up
Easy does it
Mobilise each working limb

Bend knees
Lift the spine
There's no rush, take your time

Stretch left
Stretch right
C'mon girls ain't got all night

Boost the beat
Work the heart
Stamina training, no mean part

Sweat pours
Heat rises
Drains the body, no surprises

Cool down
Shake out
Dehydrate, look about

Lie down
Tone n' trim
Squeeze bum, abdominals in

Stretch, breathe
Rest a while
Revitalise and add a smile

Do it once
Do it twice
Aerobic junkies do it thrice

Lift spirits
Get a grip
Exercise is one great trip!

Jacki Winter

WORK THAT BODY

Aerobics used to be the class of the day
Now Step seems to be the way
To work off all those cream cakes
And you a fitter person make
After Step, you can work out in the gym
Keeps you healthy and keeps you trim
Back at home carry on the good work
Keep away from foods where fat or grease lurk
If you follow a good food and exercise regime
You will be extra fit, healthy and lean.

Melanie Burgess

ENGLISH ECCENTRIC

I have seen him bathe in cold winters
Or cooled friendship, and always on form
He remains exposed, unconcerned
And jogs in his blue socks in a thunder storm.

Andrew Baily

THE VOICE

Folk laugh.
I am overweight
and love my state.
Outsize clothes upon the shelf -
a double bed all to myself.
Weight watchers is up the street
but waffles are my daily treat.

Passing my window I see:
Joggers puffing and plodding,
jarring limbs with each stride;
Teenagers in T-shirts with muscles
built by dumbbells;
Dames decked on cycles
with real pedalling power.

Why should people
intrude my world?
As long as I get food
should I care if folk are rude?
Everyone has freedom of choice
even if I hear an admonishing voice.

Caroline Frances Eyre

FITNESS FOR YOU AND ME

Johnie Cash is singing 'Lucille'
The tape is playing well today,
'Over with the left arm and touch your toes'
'Now with the right arm do the same'
Today we actually touched the floor
A month ago we could only reach a foot from our feet.
'Now jog round to your right 3 times
Then turn and go 3 times to the left.'
So off we go quite happily all of us relaxed.
'Now lie on your backs on the floor left leg in the air,
Lower slowly to the floor, and raise the right leg
Lower slowly, then raise both legs together
And lower slowly, hands behind buttocks and sit up.'
What is it all about, this keeping fit?
Already all of us feel fitter,
Most of us have lost weight, every lb. counts.
At each session we go on the scales,
'You have lost 2lb this week, very good'
'Oh what a pity, you have gained 1lb since last week
Try harder next week, you look slimmer already
Is your husband pleased dear?'
If there are heart problems in the family
It pays to look after yourself,
Have you a family relying on you?
It's so simple really, eating carefully
Doing as much exercise as possible,
As you are watching the TV, flex your fingers
Wiggle your toes, rub your hands together
We don't just owe it to other people,
But most of all to ourselves, it's our goal.

Margaret Pearce

TOMORROW

Eat more fresh fruit and vegetables too
The experts tell us this is what we should do
I want to feel better so I'll take their advice
I'll cut down on fat, sugar and salt. Starting tomorrow.

Tea, coffee, sweet fizzy drinks
All the things we like should go down the sink
Mineral water, herbal tea, that's just what we need
I'll just ground these last few beans and start tomorrow.

Increase suppleness, strength and stamina
Keep a healthy heart and please the medical examiner
A couch potato lifestyle won't keep you going
I'll take up regular exercise to keep me glowing. Starting tomorrow.

Stress, tension, it's all got to stop
Before it's too late and we grind to a halt
Relaxation, meditation, learn to wind down
I'll just meet this last deadline and start tomorrow.

Now I'm off sick, they don't know what's wrong
I've got to get back to work so I hope they don't take long
Can't find anything? What do they mean?
Surely something will show up! Perhaps tomorrow.

Two months later, they say it's stress
Listen to your body, it's sending an SOS
Symptoms are plenty, they're forming a queue
Now I've got the message, I know what to do. Starting today.

Eileen McKue

AN OBESE SENIOR CITIZEN ON AN EXERCISE BIKE

Early each morning, in the spare room,
The windows are opened.
Round go the pedals, the wheels will not budge.
Scenery stays the same,
Tame, oh so tame.
The arthritic right knee, so painful at first,
Locks and unlocks as pedals go round.

Circulating blood gets hot and hotter,
Breaths come panting, short and shorter.
Round go the pedals, the wheels are not there.
Central heating not on, even in winter.
Horses sweat, gentlemen perspire, ladies glow,
Enticing thoughts of a hot shower.

The rowing boat handlebars move to and fro,
Shoulders and arms grip with the palms.
Change the date on the calendar and cycle again.
Calories vanish . . . only in dreams.

The minutes tick by on the machine,
Achievement is less, year by year.
Is self imposed discipline good for the health?
Do old folk get mean and use what they buy?

Christ was born today; it's my birthday too,
Can I refrain, just for one day?

Kate Eggleston

THE PURSUIT OF FITNESS

I wish the experts wouldn't tell me
How to eat and exercise.
It seems to me their views today
Turn out tomorrow to be lies.

I do not aim to have a figure
A twenty-one year-old would envy.
I shall not take up step aerobics -
For me, the walk to work is plenty.

I have no wish to join the ruptured
Who wait in pain in injury clinics.
What price now their bulging biceps
As they seek attention from the duty medics?

Let others slave away at fitness,
Dress in track suit, sprint and jog.
At early morning and at evening
The most I'll do is walk the dog.

What's the point of low fat spreads?
They're full of 'Es' no, not for me.
Fat free milk's another fad -
I'll not add water to my tea.

What's wrong with full cream milk and butter?
Granny lived to ninety three,
On treacle tart and suet pudding,
Then scones with jam and cream for tea.

Suppose I want a cream eclair,
Some Belgian chocs, a plate of fries.
Some full fat cheese, a pint of beer?
And if it's not what they advise

I'll disregard the latest thinking,
Enjoy them all, and keep on drinking.

Maureen Harper

LIFE IN THE FIT LANE

Life is a long hard journey
With obstacles all the way
The very best way to travel it
Is to live it day to day.

All you can do to weather it
Is do the best you can
Staying sound in body and mind
Every woman, child and man.

First you must monitor, your intake
A healthy diet's a must
Cutting out sweets and chocolates
You'll all do this I trust.

Eat lots of fruit and vegetables
Cut down on fats and you see
Get regular and healthy exercise
And you'll *be heart trouble* free.

You know it's sound advice I give you
I'm sure you're convinced but *Gee*
I wish I could be as sensible
So tell me, how do I convince me?

Marlene Mackintosh

MRS BLOBBY

Fighting the flab,
Ten minutes on the rowing machine,
Have a drink,
It's thirsty work.

Go look in the cupboard,
Oh I can't resist,
Is it Tesco's apple and raspberry tart.

Or may be a chocolate bar,
Or a scone,
I'll work it off,
Oh this is hard work,
My willpower won't last.

Oh wibley wobley,
I'll soon look like,
Mrs Blobby.

S J Middleton

PRESCRIPTION FOR HEALTH

I've taken me garlic capsule,
I've swallowed me cod liver oil,
Taken vitamin E and Sanatogen B;
All those bugs I'm determined to foil.

I often take buttercup syrup,
Rub Vick on me chest at night,
Put a drop o'rum in me Horlicks -
I'm sure it will be alright.

I take six deep breaths every morning,
Put low fat spread on me bread.
I've cut cigs down to one every hour,
But still I feel half blinking dead.

What more can I take to reinforce me
Against all the aches and complaints?
I need nourishment that will sustain me;
I don't hold with dietetic restraints.

Perhaps if I join keep fit classes,
Exercise - work up a sweat.
I may then begin to feel better.
I'll do that - but oh! Not just yet.

S C Chambers

AN AGE TOO SOON

Fitness fads have grabbed the nation,
jogging, sport and diet.
I do not care for these at all,
so do not make me try it.

Slouching down beside the telly,
a life of food and rest.
Dreaming of a life of bliss,
this is the thing that I do best.

No jogging shorts or running shoes,
no rabbit food to eat.
No straining muscles, aching limbs,
no blisters on my feet.

Exercise is bad, bad news,
a fool will run to work.
No life of sport or healthy food,
though I'm often called a jerk.

I do not care for healthy ways,
I live a life of fun.
I'll feed myself with chips and peas,
I'll follow with cream buns.

When I leave this world behind,
these words adorn my tomb.
He left this world a happy chap,
thought it was an age too soon.

Colin Reeves

TEMPTATION

First thing in the morning
Standing on the scales
Looking at that extra pound
That added inch that tells
The story of that biscuit
The little slice of cake
Regret, why did I eat them,
It was a bad mistake.

Well, now I'll have to exercise
And really persevere,
To discipline and watch myself
Be positive, severe.
Get out my bike and peddle hard
Twice around the square,
It's going to be a lot of work
As much as I can bear.

It's evening and I'm hungry
I think I well might die
Will it make a lot of difference
If I help myself to pie?
I've always got tomorrow
I can make another start.
My word that pie was lovely,
And now I'll try the tart.

Vanda Gilbert

FIT FOR . . .

Life may expand after forty
Waistlines may get there ahead
Man may pump iron
to be viewed as a lion:
Are deltoids that useful in bed.
Now that 50 to 30 to 40
may be the ideal physique
but it can't carry clout
'cos it ain't worth a shout
for He gave the earth to the meek.

Leslie Stiles

WHEN

When I become sleek and slim,
Able to mount the stairs without loss of breath,
Or catch escaping buses,
With neither perspiration, nor untoward distress.
I shall think of what I am today,
And wonder, 'Was I ever him?'

When I'm light, alert and fast,
Impervious to pain, gaining a state of action,
Forgetting blood pressure,
And the omnipresent coronary contraction.
I'll shrug off thirty years and say,
'This is who I am at last.'

When this leaner, younger me,
Sprints the winter streets in sleet and dark,
Or lighted by my flying Nikes,
Pass ten times gasping round the park.
I shall fartlek to *The Jogger's Arms'*
Knowing where I want to be.

Dave Loomes

RESOLUTIONS

I know I'm fat, unfit and forty
And I know I really ought to
Fight the flab and watch my weight
Eat proper things, unsaturate.

But my body cries for sugar,
Begs for toffee, pleads for nougat,
Screams for cream upon my gateaux
And all the time I watch my girth grow.

But a new leaf over I will turn,
I'll join a gym, go for the burn,
I'll munch a lettuce, not a choc,
And never hear . . . 'Ahhh, what's up doc?'

Gerard Martin

EXERCISING THE IMAGINATION

I'm growing fat;
what's wrong with that?
So I'm no longer thin;
is that a mortal sin?
As I grow older
my blood runs colder
and my puny muscles spread.
But I'll not drop down dead
from a jogger's heart attack.
I don't run nowhere special
just to feel the pain
of running back.
My exercise now comes
from thinking thoughts
of pleasant sorts,
reliving memories
and impotent fantasies,
not panicking about descending bums,
the drooping breasts.
I'm at my best
at rest.

Adrian Jones

GOOD HEALTH

We are not made to while away the time
In vacant mood and idle contemplation
For we're composed of body and of mind
Designed to move in graceful application.

We must not sit and watch the world go by
Through laziness or lack of motivation
Our bodies need good food and exercise
To play its part in tune with all creation.

Just like machines made up of many wheels
All moving parts, each with a separate function
Each tiny wheel maintained and oiled and cleaned
Moves easily with effortless connection.

But if one cog, through age or just neglect
Should become stuck or cause deceleration
The whole machine may crumble to an end
Or rust away in slow disintegration.

So let us maintain our bodies and our minds
Well exercised and free from all infection
That we may give our best to all mankind
And all may reach the peak of their perfection.

Carmel Shaw

ARTHRITIS

Arthritis in my joints
alas I creak in moving parts
away to draw some solace
from the sea.
Cod liver oil is the boon for me,
four swigs from the bottle
no teaspoons now
eight years accustoms me to take
the stuff most people love to hate.

Christopher John Boden

AT THE HEALTH FARM

Floral ladies playing bridge
At a health farm for the rich -
WI's are more their scene,
Which is where they've always been.

Yet, here they are to lose some weight
And hope it will not be too late
For reform and change and eating less,
Which is causing real stress -

As they dream of bread and kippers
In the sauna wearing slippers.
Oh those salads, fruit and yog
And they're also asked to jog -

Whilst at home their spouses blithe
At the pub both drink and thrive.
When finally the wives return
With new-found zeal they hotly burn,

And hubbies expecting chips for tea
Are given lettuce leaves and brie -
So, you will no doubt agree
Divorce is rife in *Middleton-On-Sea.*

Lily Seibold

THE WALKING GAME

Miles of weekend road,
In London, Leicester or Brum,
Dodging the jogging bus,
Or the bargain hunting mum.

We filled the village halls,
With limber men and keen,
Bright with the fires of youth,
Or fragrant as winter green.

Joking, as comrades will,
To lighten the heavy miles,
We measured each others strength,
And treasured each others smiles.

No matter how tired you felt,
You'd raise a sprint for the line.
'The last man in must pay for the tea.'
'Put a sprinkle of salt in mine!'

Towelling weary limbs,
While harassed and inky men,
Compiled statistical lists,
Of who finished where and when.

And Life is a Walking game
With rules to be applied.
It's better to cross the line, my Son,
Than be disqualified.

It isn't the season's fame,
Which makes the boy a man,
It's knowing he walked in style,
And was never an also ran!

John Guy

BEFORE THE RACE

The mingled heady smells of liniment and sweat,
The shy shared edgy camaraderie
Of normally isolate strangers,
Finding their eccentricity shared
By other crackpot individuals.

The reluctant snake-like shedding of outer skin,
And the tentative first steps warming up.
Nudges of long-gone previous ills
Warn and threaten,
But the thirteen-mile journey ahead
Stretches out like a long soft carpet.

Steve Flook

NOT THE MAN I USED TO BE

In the mirror what do I see,
not the man that I used to be,
enormous hips and a big fat tum
and legs full of varicose veins.
I really must try and get fit
and start jogging round the lanes.
I'll refuse all the fatty foods
when my friends invite me to dine,
and however much they tempt me
say no to their offers of wine.
I must cut down on all things sweet
and stick to a diet of greens,
then try to get back the figure
I once had in my early teens.
I'll do press-ups every morning,
and work on the parallel bars.
I might go hiking once again
and stop riding round in cars.
Perhaps I'll buy a bicycle
and head for the open road,
to make my blood pump faster
so my arteries won't corrode.
And if by chance a talent scout
should observe me flashing by,
and pick me for the *Tour de France*
well you never know - *Pigs might fly.*

David Wicking

KEEP JOGGING!

I'm gonna run with the cars and suffer the pollution
I'm gonna lose seven pounds four weeks from now
I'm gonna exercise with my video tapes that show me how
If Madonna can have that shape, a year younger than me
Then I know it must be possible, although children I have three!
But I will not make excuses, I'm gonna make this work
I'm gonna lose this weight and stop looking like a jerk
So on with my trainers as I tie back my hair
I'm off to run a marathon, so let the neighbours stare
I'll be out there with the others, sun-bathing with them all
Wearing skimpy bikini, please let these inches fall
So when I read this back, on that hot summer's day
I wonder if it has worked, or is this fat meant to stay?

Rita Bridgman

COUCH POTATO?

I'm not a couch potato
Not yet a slim french fry.
I'm more a dash of soggy mash
With lumps that won't subside.
I'd like to be an oven chip
With five per cent less fat,
Perhaps a wisp of luscious crisp
Smooth, lean, well shaped and flat.
Duchesse or boiled potatoes
Destroy my good intention,
Plump, well cooked chips stay on my hips.
The answer is abstention!

Jean Michaels

INTERLUDE AT THE V & A RESTAURANT

I tried to feel the lady's ribs while cutting up my gateau;
She said she'd started dieting but ended on a plateau.

Aidan Baker

EXERCISE

The piercing alarm clock, it's 6am
Eyes wide open and count to 10.
Leap out of bed
Stretch and yawn.
Look out the window.
A crisp winters morn.
Track suit and trainers
Stopwatch too.
Jogging round the park
Is a good thing to do.
The piercing alarm clock, it's 6am.
Throw it away and roll over again.
A few more hours
Then you'll rise
Fall out of bed
Rub sleep from your eyes.
Toast and jam.
Mugs of sweet tea.
Slump on the sofa
Watching morning TV
Back from a jog
Shower then dress.
Exercise, they say
Relieves lots of stress
Quite happy here
I'll stay where I am.
A content couch potato
With a new jar of jam.

Tracey Jackson

METAMORPHOSIS

Bowed and shuffling, creaking, groaning,
Even notes of muffled moaning,
Is this some long forgotten rite,
Or just a strange and wondrous sight?

In time you'll see this mass emerge
With one accord they will all surge
In waves of rippling, sinew, muscle,
Lungs a bursting in the tussle.

Onward, onward fast and slow,
Racing for the goal they know.
It's not a strange and wondrous sight,
Nor a long forgotten rite.

It's fitness gathered in one place
All competing in the race.

C Hall

SHORT SPORT

Excuse my observations.
Perhaps you'll think I'm wrong.
But why does all this sport we see.
Drag on and on and on.

Why have a tennis fortnight?
I could reduce this long display
One rally each is plenty.
Then we'd have a tennis day.

And football could be shortened.
A goal kick each I'm sure would do.
The World Cup could start at 9.o'clock.
And be done by half past two.

Cricket could be an over each.
Golf one hole and no more.
And snooker why not just one frame.
You'd still finish with a score.

The savings would be enormous.
Both in energy and cost.
Time could be used constructively.
And would so much be lost?

Trevor Napper

YOGA LAMENT

I thought I'd take up Yoga
And improve my four foot ten.
Bend and stretch and touch your toes
Then do it all again.

Balance on one foot now
With arms out at the side
Keep it up don't wobble.
Laugh? I nearly died!

Roll your neck and bend your waist
But please don't bend your knees,
Stretch yourself from side to side
Then sit down if you please.

Flat upon your back now
And bring your legs up straight
Slowly, slowly bring them down
Then you can rest and wait.

Lie down prone now we are told
(Is that the front or back?)
Nose to the ground and toes turned up -
I just haven't got the knack.

Put your head down, one leg up
And put it round your neck.
I bet I'm stiff tomorrow
Golly, what a wreck.

Perhaps by then I'll change my mind
And become a couch potato,
But I'll go and have a cup of tea
And try again tomorrow.

P J Anderson

THE LAST MILE

Glowing through the gathering gloom
The cheering lights of home
How thankfully I turn the key
And flop down on the old settee.

Bill Boyle

STAYING FIT HEALTHY AND SLIM

Every day and every night
We struggle to keep our tummy's tight
To stay fit and slim and not put on an ounce
Which invariably means a *calorie count!*

Then for those more energetic than some
Various methods are tried, tested and done
Step Classes, Aerobics, Swimming, Keep Fit
Jogging, Running, still more to come yet!

Walking and dancing or a trip to the Gym
Or exercising at home *when it can fit in*
Following a book or video routine
Pleased to make an effort whilst not being seen!

Eat lots of fruit is what they all say
Plus *exercise isn't necessary every day*
Just make a small effort two or three times a week
And you may just end up with the figure you seek!

Joanne Wilding

FIT AND BROKE

You must keep fit my darling,
You must look after yourself.
Think of diet and exercise,
And start to look after your health.
There's food you can buy to stay trim dear,
Weight watchers, low calorie stuff,
You may need a two helping packet,
Cos one is just never enough.
Take a look at your life my sweet,
You need more exercise,
Try a video fitness routine,
Like Rosemary C's hip and thighs.
Or maybe some step aerobics,
Now that sounds lots of fun,
Not your cup of tea dear,
What about an invigorating run.
You could try rugby or squash love,
Or maybe a swish mountain bike.
But don't forget what ever it is,
The kit must be just right.
No you can't wear your shell suit my lover,
That's not the in thing to put on,
You need a designer label,
Anything else would be wrong.
There's Nike, Puma, and Reebok, oh and
Hi-tech, Ron Hill and Head.
After all you want to be fit and look good,
Even if your bank statement is in the red.

Janice Cowper-Smith

RACING THROUGH THE WALL

Without touching
The walls around me,
I have no meaning
In the space in between.

At my own frontiers,
I confirm
That I'm alive,
Like a mirror reflects a face.

I push,
And I push back,
Good verses bad,
Strength verses weakness.

If my will
Is not expanding
Lost miles, my will contracting
The very fighting to regain, spurs me on.

By my faith,
The pain,
The final waking as the tape breaks
The walls shall not win.

Andrew Evans

SLIMMING

I'm in a bad state
I'm two stone overweight
It's the chocolates and cakes I consume
But have I had a fright
For I looked such a sight
When I tried on my bathing costume.

No-one could desire
Me! With my spare tyre
I'm the opposite of a trend setter
And my *boobs* and my *tum*
Not to mention my *bum*
Well . . . the least said about them the better!

So I've started to slim
For I want to be trim
Now it's health foods for me from today
No *trips* to the Deli
Or snacks watching telly
And I'll get into shape come what may!

Dulcie Levene

A POEM ABOUT AGEING

As a pensioner of many years
It's easy to be submerged by fears
How can I keep fit and well,
Along these lines my thoughts do dwell.

In my minds eye
The young me is still there.
Slim of limb, firm skinned thigh
The spirit to survive in every hair.

To keep infirmity at bay
(It will not go away)
But tend to stay
A exercise plan is adhered to every day.

Before muesli, fruit, herb tea
Exercise is done to TV
A brisk walk of some duration
Lifts the spirit, it's good for motivation.

At the local library a vast choice of books
I don't forget attention to my looks
Listening to music and concerts galore
These are things I do highly adore.

Joining a Woman's Institute for a lively debate
Interest in today's world keeps me up to date
Cycling, swimming, a long ramble with a friend
Learning a language, alas my mind didn't bend.

Vitamins, fruit, greens a plenty are good for the body
I also have the occasional toddy
Above all remember if you don't use it
You will certainly loose it.

Emma K Folliard

PRIORITIES

When the priority of fitness is the goal,
The balance of multi endeavours are needs.
Whatever the star of perfection the dream,
A must is a diet that adequately feeds.
Exercise too at a leisurely pace
For the physical and for the mind
Should have regular place
Be it ballet or race,
Before success will the aspirant find.
Fed strong, and controlled
Alone will not lead
And supply all the need
For an ultimate goal of success.
For, thought has a place
Right there at the base.
Its demand positivity!
A worry or temper
Or being temperamental
Can steer off the fitness beam.
That extra bit of something
To give the glowing feeling,
Comes through the art of breathing
A deep breath of Being.

W Taylor

GOOD HEALTH

Full many a flower is born quite fair
But soon the bloom will fade
Unless it's fed and watered right
In the balance are we weighed.

You have seen, as I have too
The telltale distended belly
Of those who imbibe too much
Or watch far too much telly.

The sickly look of those sweet things
Who on sweet things waste their salaries
And eat fatty foods which cholesterol makes
To build up too many calories.

Or smoking much we all are told
Is harmful to our health
It's only good is to the Trade
Upon which it derives its wealth.

The common salt has many faults
Tho' a little we may permit
But take too much and you'll be out of sorts
And you surely won't be fit.

A lot of fruit I would suggest
For the vitamins that we lack
With fibre thrown in by the ton
To help those movements slack.

What a life I tell myself
But don't give way to despair
A balanced diet is all you need
And the bloom will re-appear.

F Selley

A HEALTHY LIFE!

When I was young and carefree
Living on a farm
Cereal, fruit and veggie
Certainly did me no harm
Walking, running, cycling, everywhere around
Good food, and fresh air abound

The middle years, oh! so fast
Husband, career, nothing I lack
Tired and working weeks go past
Children, food for everyone, I'll just snack.
Walking, running, cycling? No, a car
Slow down, slow down, I will be under par.

Holidays? Yes my vitality comes back
Grandchildren, and work ongoing
I need my supplements ACE a pack
Walking, aerobics, swimming, no knawing
Must keep active, the years roll by
Ah! retirement, I heave a sigh.

Now I am *old* and carefree
And living on a hill
Cereal, fruit and veggie
I take my fill
Walking, aerobics, swimming and more
With my supplements, I will meet whatever life has in store.

Ida M Maguire

THE PAVILION

I can be there again in a moment. Autumn
Shingling the red-gold beeches, a distant mouth of river
Incoherent with flood. In front of the pavilion
A hundred rugby studs, blue and red jerseys
MacGregor walking back and forwards at the front
His blue eyes cold as sky. Someone breaks out laughing
The hawk stabs, plucks and eats. My heart's a leaping stone
But every finger bloodless - in a moment they will stumble at a ball
Blind and dead, the nerves too tight. The poplars rush with coins
October light comes down across the grass in yellow pools
The sun still loves us, even for a moment then MacGregor stands
Drenched in a golden fire and cannot speak.
A thousand times I'd heard him kick at boys, the vicious mouth
Twisted with abuse; I'd seen the leather belt slash down at hands
The power bleeding from his eyes, but now
He cannot speak, he turns away and is a child
Before a greater God. All the Autumn rushes, jumps in fire
The chestnuts break, the water silvers in the hills
And I know in myself that I am still alive and free.

Kenneth C Steven

TAP FOR FITNESS

Aerobics, Step, I tried them all,
At home, in halls, at evening school,
Tap dance now I want to do,
Keeps you fit and supple too.

Tap for 40 + and more,
All us oldies take to the floor,
Tapping toes and clicking heel,
Just so we can get the feel.

Shuffle says the teacher now,
Oh I do wish I knew how,
What will she make us do next?
Now I feel a little vexed.

Double treble timesteps long,
Me I usually do it wrong,
Shuffle hop step do it right,
Or we will be here all night.

We persevere my friends and I,
Oh golly how hard we do try,
Practise hard both fast and slow,
Our teacher says, let's do a show.

Routine planned and music picked,
I do hope this don't get me licked,
Practise, practise night and day,
Nothing will get in my way.

The day has come to do our bit,
I am so nervous must admit,
The show went well, so fast I'm wheezy,
My next venture has got to be easy.

R Seward

FANATIC

I religiously attend,
At eight each Friday night,
To lose a few more pounds,
Is the aim of my fight.

Within minutes you'll find me
Sweating and smelling,
My arms and legs tired,
But bulging and swelling.

Mere minutes it takes,
To get me in pain.
But once I've fought into my lycra,
I can then start to train.

Adrian Dowrick

LOSING

Fit at fifty -
What a hope.
Overweight -
On chocolate choke.
Must try at least -
Reduce the feast;
Eat apples, fish,
Reject each fatty dish.
Every day
Walk briskly
Round the park
In light or dark.
Exercise
By noon or night,
Knees bend,
Arms swing.
To the end,
That's the thing;
Scales tip,
Pounds lost;
Now really fit,
But, Oh, the cost.

Jannette Golding

EXERCISE

Exercise your right to be free,
Democracy is no longer democratic,
Freedom of speech, operational, free,
Ignored by our governments epileptics,
Idiocy; foaming right down to the knee,
Taxation now cripples our country,
Poverty rears its ugly head,
We're trying to keep ourselves healthy,
Exercise?

Truth that's turned into fable,
Lies turning white into black,
I think we are no longer able,
To stay healthy, under their flack,
Fat with their poisonous labels,
Exercise?

Exercise your right to be free,
Screaming out justice for peace,
MPs won't even listen,
New laws on literature on lease,
That is their final decision,
Character assassination, one spouts with defiance,
Funny; nothing in his life is sane,
The gentleman owns, nothing but annoyance,
Exercise?

Militants forced behind bars,
A situation cut off from our view,
Back to basics, they count the stars,
Then plaster graffiti all over the loo,
Pumping iron, muscles against lies,
Exercise?

George Livingston Shand

HEALTHY STEPS

I reflect for an hour I have been in a trance
As I listened to instructions, music step dance.
March it out, Grapevine, quick as a wink
No chance to ponder, stop or to think.
Wide, wide, narrow, single, single, double
Whoops, the woman in front has got in a muddle.
Arms, legs, movements, must keep going
As the change of direction keeps flowing.
The pace now changing, a wind down for the heart
Two digs to the left, cooling down now must start.
Slowly, slowly, marching, the end of an hour
Where all have blossomed like many a flower.
Aerobics is healthy and great fun
Aerobics is geared for just everyone.

Gwenyth E Jones

LET'S DANCE

Dancing classes twice a week
Is all I need to reach my peak.
Stretch N' Dance The class is called and it's
Open to all if you dare to call.

Gently stretching we all begin
Lengthening our bodies we find keeps us trim.
Every part of the body is awakened as
Energy flows from our heads down to our toes.

The central area of the body is our focus
We aim to work from a strong, firm centre.
Using this as our stable base
We discover we can move with unlimiting grace.

So many movements are discovered and tried
Twisting and turning and jumping astride.
Testing our balance we reach to one side,
Rise from a plié and pivot in time.

To strengthen and tone
We try some yoga moves
Can we reach up and over and down?
We never could before . . .

We dance our learnt routine
To jazz or funk or Queen.
Our blood flows, our skins glow
As we dance our last dance tonight

The taste of Astaire is always there
In every step and move
So who can resist the chance to dance
Since to dance is to love and to *live*!

Joan Webster

THE PAIN BARRIER

When I was young I used to run
For miles without a pain.
Every day I'd plod away
(Apart from in the rain).
But at the age of fifty-two, I knew
That I would never run again.

I'd hurt my knee, you see,
Through over-exercise.
The pain, sometimes so intense,
Brought tears into my eyes.
My elbow also gave me pain
Due to an old mountaineering strain,
Not to mention my lower back,
For every time that I bent down
I sort of heard it crack.

But with gentle massage every day at four,
My back is back, the way it was, back before.
And my knee? Well that feels so much better
Ever since the doctor gave me a letter.

My arm still hurts, occasionally it's true
But I've started doing press-ups
Very carefully, just a few.
And I'm not joking, I've stopped smoking
And I've started running, too.

When I was fifty-two, I absolutely knew
That I would never run again.
But now I'm fifty-four,
And I can run much further
Than I ever could before,
Even in the rain.

John Merritt

SINGLES NIGHT AT THE SWIMMING POOL

Love is swimming in a pool of
Almost naked strangers.
You can fall in or be pushed;
Dive from the highest board or
Edge self-consciously into the shallow end.
Maybe you feel out of condition,
Or maybe you're there to show off
Your muscles or your breaststroke:
It hardly matters: it's one of those skills you
Never forget once you learn it,
However infrequently you exercise.
You can take lessons or pick it up as you go along,
Taking all precautions not to drown.
It can begin as a weekly affair and
End up an addiction,
Indulged in both morning and night,
Though some try once and then say
Never again, having suffered cramp or injury.
Some take part as an Olympic sport,
Others just for pleasure or to keep in trim.
You can synchronise your strokes with several partners
Or set distance above grace and style,
Persisting to see how many lengths you'll do.
Someday perhaps you can learn to lifesave too;
Maybe then you can cast aside the water wings
Advised to you for safety,
And hope that, when it's
Singles night at the local swimming pool,
Your fellow swimmer will become
Your life-preserver.

Caragh Devlin

A BIT OF WHAT YOU FANCY

Every now and then
When I've had a binge again
I dive into a health-kick diet
Sugary or fat then I won't buy it.

Free-range, whole and organic fare
I grab my basket and I am there
Grains and pulses don't stand a chance
When I and my empty jars advance.

Feeling better already and fighting fit
Hair so shiny, no nasty zits
I take a walk to enhance the flow
Spot a Mars bar in a shop, Oh No.

Linda Yantolo

FANATICALLY HEALTHY

I start the day with a milk bath,
Rosemary, citrus or pine,
I wake to the power of ginseng
With muscle tone for my spine.

I take acidophilus culture
And am really happy to know
That so many friendly bacteria
Give my insides a rosy glow.

My multivitamin capsules
Give me the boost I need,
Along with cod liver oil
And a dose of crushed seaweed

Daily Beta Carotene
Gives me a golden tan.
Oil of orchid and Devil's Claw
Are part of my healthy lifeplan.

Alfalfa sativa tablets
Have a beneficial effect,
And Greenland shark capsules,
I think I'll try those next.

And yet, despite all my efforts,
I'm probably misunderstood,
For at the end of the day,
I've no money left for food!

Brian Moses

WISE LIVING

No I am not a fitness fanatic,
But I may be called a lunatic.
Being very selective what I eat.
The last ten years I've cut out meat.

Two cooked meals a day I make
Nothing fancy like puds or cake
Cheese, fish and plenty of greens
Plus onions, garlic and runner beans.

I do a full day's work, no physical jerks.
Eat plenty of honey, a must for my money.
Have a voluntary post of mental kind
At eighty-five I am alert in mind

Able in body with my own bottom teeth
I shall not yet be ordering my personal wreath
Hope to go on for a year or two more
It's nice to feel well not a family bore.

H G Irvine

LIVING WELL!

Fit and fancy free! The best of all worlds.
Balancing lifestyles, with body and brain:
Health is part of a multifaced frame:
One small part can weaken the chain.

Stress can erupt in physical boils,
Dangers of life still threaten the spoils.
Yes! Care for the body, but also the head -
Don't over-eat, nor end up brain dead!

All have to work to our greatest extent,
Yet not a drop more; Allowing time spent
To balance our lives; To nurture the spirit
Plus body and brain: In total, be fit.

Jan

HEALTH AND FITNESS

Health and fitness is the way
To have the good-life every day
It's as good for me as it is for you
And everyone, everywhere, can enjoy it too

All it takes is willpower and dedication
To avoid ill health and termination
Eating and doing all the right things
Will help to prevent an early set of wings

What you eat is very important indeed
So monitor your intake and take heed
Many a person has eaten the wrong food
If you eat the right things, you'll look good in the nude!

Everything in our lives usually comes with a price
Hard work, discipline of exercise will make you feel nice
Remember that health and fitness go hand in hand
All of us can get involved, without spending a grand!

Take the first steps, it's easy you'll see
The compliments from others will fill you with glee
Do all of these things as they're good for the heart
And you'll be sure that mind, body and spirit, are less likely to part!

Trevor I Bale

HOLISTICALLY SPEAKING

A holistic approach to health I find
Is the best there is for body and mind.
The physical and emotional aspects can
Improve the total body of woman and man.

And so, I try the following approach
Upon my enjoyment I do not encroach.
For fitness is fun in all its different ways
Through exercise and diet, there is a message always.

Instead of driving my car I cycle my bike
And replace my bus rides by taking a hike.
I enjoy a game of badminton and tennis too
These are my favourite sports, to name but a few.

I've also changed from white bread to brown
And eat fruit and veg without a frown.
Trim the fat off meat, grill instead of frying
It's easy to keep healthy without really trying.

A good intake of water, eight glasses per day
Helps skin and digestion, keeps troubles at bay.
Reading labels informs me of the value of food
Both nutritious and calorific giving me the right to choose.

Relaxation and meditation effectively combine
To soothe the body and helps me unwind.
Adequate sleep keeps me feeling alert and bright
Seven or eight hours is necessary every night.

So, this is my approach to maintaining a healthy existence
It's really quite enjoyable, I aim to be consistent
I feel very well and can honestly say
The *Holistic approach is the only way.*

Y M Wright

SHAPING UP

Used to drive around,
Feeling generally run down,
Used to take deep breaths as I did ride,
Filled my lungs with Carbon Monoxide.
When, reluctantly, I left my wheels,
I'd sit behind a desk or a television with cans,
an ashtray and take-away meals.

One day I got a twinge, a kind of pain.
The Doctor said 'Sir, this lifestyle's insane!'
My brush with death filled me with fear.
I decided there and then I had to get fit, move up a gear.
Started easily, I knew that was the way.
Ate carefully, three straight meals a day.
Amidst ridicule, I declared to my colleagues,
'Watch the change in a year!'

Walk . . . run, walk . . . run,
At first I did it of necessity, then for fun.
My breathing improved, sleeping too -
My friends asked, 'Is that really you?'
Weights, Aerobics, Step and Rebounding,
Soon I found that no longer my heart was pounding,
Just my muscles and veins, strain lifted,
everything was so much easier to do.

At forty, I feel better than ever before,
Getting through the day is no longer a war.
I don't need to fight against tiredness, or battle for breath,
But this only happened after coming face to face with death.
I could have gone on struggling, living life at half-speed.
Now *you* can do the same, you'll feel the change as you
fulfil the need.
Nothing to stop you, so do it now. Moving, Breathing,
Living . . . Shaping up.

Nick Leather

AGE OF FITNESS

Pumping iron - Hatha Yoga,
Football, cricket, volleyball
Treadmill treading, rowing madly
Scaling up the rung clad wall.
Acupuncture, Ayuveda
Vits. and tonics by the score
Raja Yoga, meditation
Not quite knowing what's in store
Exercising great precaution
Over drink and diet too
When I pause and think about it
'Tis hell I've put my body through!
Has it kept me fit and healthy
Well - I suppose I'm still alive
And it's in my genes I reckon
That I need to *do* to thrive
Mind it's slightly irritating
That my smoking, beery friends
Couch potatoes, fish and chippies
Think that I am round the bend
They seem fit and very happy
Without contorting every joint
And as they stroll through life quite sweetly
I often wonder *What's the point* -
Then that devil thing inside me
Says *You've got to keep in trim*
I shudder gently - then quite docile
Off I trot down to the gym!
There - lithe bodies - gently sweating
Deep inside me - *This is heaven*!
I'd love to come down here more often
Even though I'm seventy-seven!

John Elias

FITNESS POEM

I haven't got time for aerobics
Too frenetic you see
Jogging makes me breathless
Weight training isn't for me

I eat a healthy diet
With lots of fruit and veg
When I haven't got my bus fare
I walk to the shops instead

I walk and walk and walk
Twelve miles a week or more
It doesn't make me weary
Nor do my feet get sore

Walking raises my spirits
I can stop and smell the flowers
I can listen to beautiful bird song
I can be outside for hours

It's my favourite form of exercise
I neither swim nor ride a bike
So I just put on my shoes
And I go out for a hike.

Kathy Richardson

DOUBLE VISION

I'm a person who takes an intelligent interest in diet and health.
You're a wacky *food and fitness* health fanatic.
I'm someone who prefers Food without Cruelty, or chemicals
You're a veggie nutcase with a sentimental and
unrealistic attitude towards animals.
I believe in taking something to help redress the
disbalance to my system from the unhealthy eating
habits of a society based on conspicuous consumption.
You're a health supplement pill junkie - and a long-winded prig!
I'm a gentle jogging, swimming and yoga enthusiast
who's a naturally early-riser.
You're a sadomasochistic, get-up-and-go, insomniac,
who terrifies all the cats and dogs in the neighbourhood
in his quest for a dubious immortality.

In short: *I am what I eat and how I use this body* and know it.
You are what you eat and how you use that body - and don't.
Who, then are we?

Richard Parkhurst

FIGHTING THE FLAB

Upsadaisy - out of bed
And a few deep breaths
A few pelvic lifts
On the bathroom floor
After getting on those scales!

Stretch
Up and across
Breathe out

Down for breakfast
Herbal medicine first
In warm water
It tastes only a little bitter
Said to affect nerves in throat
With direct path to the liver

Got to get rid of those gallstones
Get the fat moving
Stirring in my body

So as to lose it and gain
New youthfulness and vitality
Or at least retain
Flexible joints and a bouncy step
For my long walk to work and home again.

Jane Pietrusiak

SCALES TELL TALES

Suddenly my heart sings
Takes wings
Spirits soar
What is more
I am happy.

Oh the months
That I have tried
Nearly cried
Only sighed
Yet self-denied.

What is more
Things I adore
Never came
Within my door
Cupboard or fridge.

Down from twenty
Seventeen, sixteen too!
Cast offs plenty
Yet not blue
All clothes new.

Younger in heart
With body change
Now I've stopped
My wicked ways
And slimmed!

Doreen Shand

IT DOESN'T COME EASY

It doesn't come easy for me to keep fit
I'm naturally lazy and to this I admit
It's Saturday morning and I'd rather just lay
But I know a tornado is heading my way
Blaring music and a screeching of brakes
Guarantees all my neighbours awake
Down to the gym with my brother I go
As it doesn't come easy for me to say no
He talks of giving yourself the right fuel
Proper nutrition is the golden rule
We work out gently till our bodies are warm
Oh it doesn't come easy for me to perform
I try and hide my bodies distress
And complete my sets on the bench press
It isn't easy but I thought it was great
When he only pushed six times but still counted eight
Both of us now are feeling the strain
Our muscles are tiring with increasing pain
The Pec-Deck the arm curl then onto our legs
The clock confirms that there's no time left
Now I'm so pleased that I didn't just lay
Roll over and waste my Saturday
It didn't come easy but now I don't care
I really feel good like I'm walking on air.

Martin Rich

SWIMMING

Trapped behind an office desk
In Mammon's iron hands,
I must exhaust my body
To free and calm my mind.

To swim
Is to purge the mind
And smooth away the ugly scars
Of daily office grind,

To free the soul to rise above
The confines of a dreary world:
And so, I swim.

Heather Woolley

MY PUNISHING REGIME

I rise very early each morning
And on natural muesli I dine
Jog to the baths, swim forty lengths
And arrive at work before nine

At ten o'clock in the morning
Whilst my colleagues choose chocolate for their snack
I opt for fruit and bottled water
I don't want to risk heart attack!

It's usually salad at lunch time
As I endeavour to keep myself trim
Then before arriving home in the evening
I stop for an hour at the gym

I'm having a struggle giving up coffee
It's quite an addiction for me
I've bought lots of boxes from the health store
Of all different flavoured herbal tea!

8 pm finds me working out with Mr M
Whilst lying full length on the floor,
I breathe in at the count of two
Then out at the count of four

I even joined a local dancing class
But that was impossible to master
After only two classes, unfortunately
I ended up with my leg in plaster

You probably think I've gone fitness mad
And laugh at my punishing regime
But I'll be the one that laughs longest
When I'm transformed into a lean machine.

Brenda Scully

THE GENTLE ART OF YOGA

I'm getting no younger, I'm sorry to say.
So what do I do to keep wrinkles at bay,
To stop muscles sagging, to keep spirit calm?
The answer is Yoga - which does good, never harm.

I've selected my book and my leotard's bought,
I am learning control for each movement and thought.
Good breathing is vital and needs concentration,
It steadies and quietens and brings relaxation.

The poses when practised correct body's ills
Thus rarely resorting to potions and pills.
No more spinal stiffness, with the cobra and plough,
The pose of the archer - the head of a cow.

For confidence, poise, try the eagle or tree.
For fatigue or bad memory, the bow - head to knee.
Too heavy? Lethargic? Try the spinal twist pose,
For asthma - the headstand, and so on it goes.

Sitting cool and erect in the lotus position
I try meditation and thinking transition.
Learning how to transpose a young face over mine,
Defining the jaw - and erasing each line.

I'm finding great peace, as a flower I create
In my mind, free from worries and in meditative state.
Then transporting myself to a favourite place
To escape to, whenever life's going at a pace.

There is no competition, and age is no bar,
You go at your own pace, just as *you* are.
I hope that it's working, I hope I am winning
For to me Yoga heralds a great new beginning.

I'm glad I decided to take up this art,
I'm more positive now and I feel young at heart.

S Gargett

HAPPY HEALTHY AND FIT

I know they regard me as a bit of a crank
And for that I don't blame them, to be quite frank.
No meat, no sweets nor fizzy drink,
The place for coffee is down the sink.
I have no use for frying pans
Nor processed food from out of cans.
Fresh fruit and veg, herbs, nuts and rice
Are all I need - they will suffice
To keep me healthy, free from ills,
I have no need of doctor's pills.
My message kit of essential oils
Relax, refresh, from all lifes toils.

My pleasures are simple for keeping fit
(I have no time to sit and knit).
For expensive classes are not for me
In stuffy rooms - I must be free
To walk, to cycle, to go for a swim
No need have I for a sweaty gym.
I tend my herbs, my roses and veggies
And mow the lawn and cut the hedges.
I do not smoke nor go out *beering*,
I have no use for power steering.
So for health and happiness it's plain to see
You don't have to be wealthy to keep fit like me.

Wendy Carmody

FITNESS FAD?

Who's fit as a fiddle, hale as can be?
Who's tough as old leather?
You've guessed it - it's me!

Not plump as a partridge nor heavy as lead,
Like the time I was so fat
I crashed right through the bed.

No, I'm flat as a flounder and I feel right as rain.
I'm light as a feather
'Cause I'm at it again.

I jog every morning, I'm up with the lark.
I go swimming each day,
Take the dog to the park.

I eat fresh fruit and fibre and vitamin C
And when I look in the mirror
I marvel at me!

But in bed in my nightmares as I run, dance and skip,
I can feel myself flagging
And I don't feel so hip

In those dreams I return to my life as a slouch,
Watch TV and eat chocolates
On my comfy old couch.

When I wake full of guilt I wonder in fear,
Will my fitness fad last
Till the end of the year?

Ilonka David

DIET BLUES

It's time to get in shape again
And start with exercise and pain
Back to the diet of healthy grub
No more ice-cream by the tub

I'll walk the dog and wash the car
And jog down to my local Spar
I'll take an attitude that's right
I know I can win this fight

Happy-go-lucky and full of health
I won't need material wealth
I'll wake one day to find the strife
Has become my way of life

The body perfect reigns supreme
It doesn't have to be a dream
A state of mind is what I need
I'm determined to succeed.

Heather Newman

BLOOD SWEAT AND TEARS

Aerobics, weight training, jogging
The thought of them sets me sobbing
Good for you
I don't buy it, but
Did once go
On a diet.

Swimming's fine
Tennis taboo
My eating's healthy
Drinking too

You may be full
Of airs and graces
So - all your bits
Fit the right places

When your exhausted
And passed on
I'll still be here
Calorie counting
Never fear

I may not be *super gran*
Contented with my *bod*
I am
Judge not the book by its cover
It may not entice a
Lover wealthy

But it sure *feels good* sure *feels healthy.*

Teresa White

FULL HOLIDAY REGIME

Who wants to wear a bikini anyway?
Sitting straight to stop a role from showing
No time allowed for slouching
Finer days and skimpy shorts,
Slight press to inner thigh.
Lighter still the tightening of the bum
Does it matter anyway with heat and sun
we bloat a little.
Odd glance from native ageing lady
at my cheeky shorts.
I had a little chuckle with
added grin nearly thinking aloud
Madam you never had these legs at any age.
The odd wave of the arm,
a stretch here and there.
Outer press on lower limbs
when one thinks of sun and heat,
shorts in Greece,
and a full set bathing suit.

Margaret Spanos

FITNESS FANATIC OR AT EASE WITH MYSELF

Am I a fitness fanatic?
Not any more
I started with jogging,
Bought the right kind of gear,
Went out in all weathers,
But my knees complained and my ankles collapsed.
So I went to the gym.
Felt good everyday,
Cycling on the static bike
Challenged by the machines.
It was fun for a while,
But after a few months
My blood pressure began to rise.
So I thought I would swim.
But the pool was either too crowded
Or closed when I had the time.
So I walked instead.
But the streets and the parks are not safe.
Too many muggings and rapes.
So now I sit and relax
Take massage for my aching muscles.
Reflexology to nurture all zones.
They give me a cup of herb tea when I am finished.
More civilised I say.
No more a fitness fanatic,
No sweating body or injured limbs.
I chose comfort for my care
And fitness within.

Josephine Blyth

MY WAY

Do I exercise every day?
Depends on what you mean.
To go out jogging or the gym,
Is really not my scene.
I get a sort of workout,
Almost every day.
But not in the excepted sense.
I do it all, my way,
I bend to do the vacuuming,
I stretch to peg out clothes,
My weight consists of shopping bags,
Extremely heavy loads.
It's all so cost effective,
Infact, it's all for free.
The bonus of a tidy house,
With a fit and healthy me.
Most diets are expensive.
Big business starts a trend,
It all boils down to commonsense.
Acceptance in the end.
I think I'm just a realist,
Eat badly now and then.
And face the fact, a size sixteen -
Will never, be a ten . . .

June Fricker

NEW IMAGE

In years gone by - I must be fair,
I was the *tortoise*, not the *hare*.
Young though I was I had to pass
From seeing my form in the looking glass.
Too many cakes and buns it's true,
It had to stop - but what to do?
Until while watching my TV
I saw the way to a fitter me.
Mr Motivator was his name.
Teaching keep fit was his game
His exercises were tough - but fun.
In time to music I tightened my tum.
By working hard on legs and knees
Soon I found I could move with ease.
Toning muscles in upper arms
Helped reveal my long lost charms,
Combined with diet light and fruity
Daily I would do my duty.
Up and down, and in and out
My legs and arms would fly about.
After just a few more weeks
I felt I had almost reached my peak!
There in the mirror I could see
A slimmer, happier little me!
No longer needing chocolate pud
Because I felt so well, so good!
Now when dressed in latest mode
So *chic* I could appear in *Vogue*
Now 'Mirror Mirror on the wall
Who is the fairest one of all?'

Alexandra

UNTITLED

Aerobics mean a lot to me,
They really make me thrive,
High impact, low impact, stepping out,
I really feel Alive.

I'd like to spread the word around,
Tell others if they would
Just make that extra effort,
They really would feel good.

The age you are, the shape you are,
It really does not matter,
You'll soon find out, to your delight,
You will feel so much better.

Your limbs may ache initially,
Your face a little red,
But don't give in, it is worthwhile,
Be positive instead.

S Nelson

A VITAMIN FOR BREAKFAST

A vitamin for breakfast and a laxative for dinner
A rub down with a kernel scrub, no wonder I look thinner.
A seaweed bath, a toothpaste, made from something quite unique
And a moisturising face wash fished from somewhere up the creek.
A capsule full of garlic, that ensures you can't go wrong
But forgets to kindly mention that you'll end up with a pong
Something to make your hair grow, even if you've just a strand,
Containing something deadly, though the product isn't banned.
A pill if you're a female, a lozenge if a male
They have the same ingredients but thereby hangs a tale!
A cream if you've got eczema and a rub if you've got gout
I wish there was a tablet that could sort the whole lot out.
But until there is I'll suffer and continue with a course,
Of a powdered natural product recommended for a horse.
Proceeding with a routine guaranteed to train an army
But wait I'm only kidding, I'm not that blooming barmy.

David Whitney

CALLING SENIOR CITIZENS

With captivating brevity,
With scintillating levity,
Herewith, to every OAP
I give my fitness recipe.

Supplements, in moderation
Are worthy of your veneration.
Vit C, will often check a threatened cold.
Fibre helps the inward parts,
Garlic makes for healthy hearts,
A and D are worth their weight in gold.

Shun all the additives you can,
Follow a healthy diet plan.
Think positively all along the way;
Play lots of bowls, take country strolls,
And count your blessings every single day.

W Price

STEP AEROBICS

Feet apart,
Knees slightly bent,
This is how my free time is spent.

Step, touch,
Feet fully on the box,
Feeling the vibrations go thro' my socks.

Stretched abs,
Release those ribs,
Who invented women's limbs?

Circle round,
Roll on down,
Resembling a circus clown.

Punch it,
Both hands - a heal,
By this time, man, the pain is real!

Travel,
Bend the legs,
What! Those now wooden pegs?

Reach,
Single swing,
Please! Can I stop this thing?

Thirsty!
You can tell?
I could drink a whole damn well!

Tired?
And sick?
Gruesome, that Step Aerobic!

Dawn O'Hanlon

THE AEROBIC GROUPIE

With sports bag on shoulder and trainers on feet,
It's down to the gym where aerobic groupies meet.
Squeeze into a lycra, whilst taking deep breaths,
Sweat bands at the ready, there's no time to rest.
Trip into the studio, (damn those laces)
Where teacher is ready to put us through our paces.
Music blares out, it's time to warm up,
With grapevines, shoulder shrugs, marches and step touch.
Muscles are stretched, the body awakes,
Let jogging commence, hope nothing will break!
We sweat grunt and groan, but never do moan,
We're high on energy and our bodies we tone.
Jogging now over, it's onto the floor.
But not to rest up, oh yes there is more!
Bums and tums to be worked and pelvic floor thrusts.
Some pectoral squeezes will improve sagging busts.
Rover's revenge (legs cocked at an angle of 90 degrees)
Just like male doggies when ready to pee.
The cool down begins, with a few cat coils,
Backs arched up like moggies, but no more need we toil.
It's time to relax and stretch out worked muscles,
Smug in the knowledge that we're fit for life's bustle.

Jenny Hall

A GOOD INTENTION

I picked up a keep-fit video,
To go with my keep-fit gear,
I thought I'd make the effort to keep in shape,
Like I do - once a year.

As soon as I arrived back home,
I started right away,
Huffing and puffing, arms in the air,
Did I really have to do this today?

First my left leg, then my right,
I'm out of breath in no time,
Why does it feel like I'm being punished,
For some horrible, dastardly crime?

But I started so now I must finish,
This hellish and foolish charade,
Though surely I've done enough for today,
But I still feel like a big lump of lard.

It's this stupid outfit, I can't get it on,
It doesn't seem to fit me at all,
Though it doesn't exactly make life easy,
When it happens to be two sizes too small!

F M Mitchell

THE RUNNER'S DANCE

Slowly grace, skill of rhythm, dance begins to formalise
Concentrate on my breathing, the dual polarities harmonise
Hard run, soft run, just run, Zen run, whirl and twirl in sufi trance
High intoxication, exhilaration, knowing that it will enhance.

The weaving lines of cosmic loom, it's all a dance and not a sport
Perfect means within the game, perfect balance on the court
I seek the game that goes forever, I want the play and not the pay
Floating Tao, game of space-time, hoping that *now* will stay.

A metaphor of microscopic, the metaphor of macaronis
There is a focus I can adjust, to the level of higher consciousness
I turn the dial, it begins to clear, having seen, having read
No need for muscles or a body, it all goes on inside my head.

I feel the ground beneath the air, that's beneath my running feet
Softly gliding through the vision, that stirs the serpent from it's seat
Rising higher through the doorways, seeking access to the light
Kunderlini, serpent power, cosmic forces, cosmic night.

Runners high, runners dream, running freely, through the wall
Mindfulness of mindfulness, empty space where I can fall
To the centre of the cyclone, where at last I am myself
Exercise of physical nature, exercise my spiritual health.

M Cossington

DUST

They tell me
that the dust
that settles in my flat
is mostly made up
of dead skin
I must have cleaned up
my whole body by now
but it's still not keeping
me thin.

Ian Russell

A HEALTHY MIND . . .

Indulgence,
Mindless trolley shopping,
Stretch and flex my muscles
Till indistinctness clears.

Hungers,
Displayed upon my frame,
Propel me through the water
Till I absolve my fear.

Banalities
In type-cast re-enactments
Make me run
Till I and they are of the air.

Hanne Olsen

IT ONLY SEEMS LONGER!

Where are all the health freaks who want to live forever?
They jog before breakfast then eat small portions of fibre
Disguised as oats and cereal.
They wash down their brown bread with fruit juice
And bottled water from effervescent spas
Before brushing their teeth with pure bristle.
Shunning cigarettes and smoky atmospheres
They sit on park benches with cottage cheese lunches
Exercising deep breathing.
Salad and vitamin pills complete their day
Before they lie in air filled rooms with open windows
Dreaming of excitement.
Where are they?
How is it they look so normal, escaping recognition?
Doesn't it all work?

Catherine Riddell

FIT-NESS

I've always known that I was rather odd
The other kids at school made that quite plain.
But just what marked me out I could not tell -
Till, late in life, one night I had a fit.

Teaching a class of kids was still allowed
But driving to the school was now outlawed.
My life was ruled by very powerful drugs
Which turned me from a man into a mouse.

What should I do? I looked both high and low
For something that would help relieve my state.
I read, took tests, consulted medicos,
Doctors and books and tests said much the same.

Fitness, they reckoned, would soon make me well.
Weights, yoga, walks and biking worked a treat!
The irony of this you should not miss
To get away from fits, you must be fit!

Donne James Buck

INFORMATION

We hope you have enjoyed reading this book - and that you will continue to enjoy it in the coming years.

If you like reading and writing poetry drop us a line, or give us a call, and we'll send you a free information pack.

Write to

Poetry Now Information
1-2 Wainman Road
Woodston
Peterborough
PE2 7BU.